MARK SAGUOR

The LLC on a Budget

How to Start Your Business Without Breaking the Bank

Contents

Preface

Congratulations on taking the first step towards your entrepreneurial dream! This book, "The LLC on a Budget: How to Start Your Business Without Breaking the Bank," is your roadmap to navigating the exciting yet often-daunting world of launching a Limited Liability Company (LLC) with limited funds.

We'll explore the benefits of choosing an LLC structure, while keeping a watchful eye on costs. We'll delve into the world of free and low-cost resources to help you navigate the legal and tax complexities of forming your business. But this book goes beyond just the formation process. We'll equip you with strategies for keeping your overhead low throughout the life of your business, from finding affordable workspaces to leveraging free marketing techniques.

Most importantly, we'll cultivate a resourceful and resilient mindset – the hallmark of a successful bootstrapper entrepreneur. So, are you ready to turn your passion into a thriving business, all while keeping your budget happy? Let's begin!

1

Building Your Foundation on a Budget

A. Why Choose an LLC? (Benefits and Considerations)

Congratulations! You've decided to embark on the exciting journey of entrepreneurship. But before you dive headfirst into product development and marketing strategies, there's a crucial first step: choosing the right business structure.   This sub-chapter will explore why a Limited Liability Company (LLC) might be the perfect fit for your budget-conscious startup.

Limiting Your Liability, Protecting Your Assets: One of the most significant advantages of an LLC is limited liability protection. This legal shield separates your personal assets (like your car or house) from the business's assets. If your business encounters financial difficulties or gets sued, your personal belongings are generally safeguarded. This provides peace of mind, allowing you to take calculated risks without jeopardizing your financial security.

Tax Advantages: Avoiding Double Taxation:
LLCs offer another perk – pass-through taxation. This means the business itself doesn't pay income tax. Instead, the profits or losses of the LLC "pass through" to the individual members on their personal tax returns. This eliminates the burden of double taxation, which occurs when a corporation pays taxes on its profits, and then shareholders pay taxes again on the dividends they receive.

Management Flexibility: Tailoring the Structure to Your Needs
An LLC provides flexibility in how you manage your business. Unlike a corporation with a rigid structure, you have the freedom to decide whether the members themselves will manage the LLC or appoint managers to handle day-to-day operations. This control allows you to structure the business in a way that best suits your needs and goals.

Considerations: Understanding the Limitations
While LLCs offer numerous advantages, it's essential to be aware of their limitations. For instance, attracting investors can be more challenging with an LLC compared to a corporation. Additionally, some states might impose annual fees on LLCs.

Is an LLC Right for You?

An LLC is an excellent choice for many entrepreneurs, particularly those who are cost-conscious and prioritize protecting their personal assets. However, the ideal business structure depends on your specific circumstances. Consider factors like the number of owners, your growth potential, and your long-term financial goals.

Next Steps:

Now that you have a better understanding of the benefits and considerations of an LLC, we'll delve deeper into the formation process in the next sub-chapter. We'll explore the associated costs and help you decide whether tackling the process yourself or seeking professional help is the most cost-effective option for your LLC.

B. Understanding the Costs of Forming an LLC (State Fees, Registered Agent Services)

So you've decided an LLC is the perfect structure for your startup. Now it's time to crunch some numbers and understand the associated costs. While forming an LLC is generally less expensive than incorporating a business, there are still some fees to consider.

State Filing Fees:

The biggest expense you'll encounter is the state

filing fee.   This fee varies significantly by state, ranging from a low of $50 to upwards of $500. You can find the specific filing fee for your state by visiting the website of your Secretary of State's office.

Registered Agent Services:

Every LLC requires a registered agent. This is an individual or service that agrees to receive legal documents on behalf of your business, such as service of process or annual reports. While you can act as your own registered agent, it might not be ideal for everyone. Registered agent services typically charge a yearly fee, ranging from $30 to $300 depending on the provider.

Optional Expenses:

There are additional costs to consider,   though they're not mandatory. These include:

- **Publication Costs:** In some states, you may be required to publish a notice of your LLC formation in a local newspaper. These fees can vary depending on the publication.
- **Business Licenses and Permits:** Depending on your industry and location, you might need specific licenses or permits to operate your business. These fees can vary widely.
- **EIN (Employer Identification Number):** While not mandatory for all LLCs, obtaining an EIN can simplify tax filing and opening business bank

accounts. There is no fee to apply for an EIN
from the IRS.

Cost-Saving Strategies:
Here are some tips for minimizing the formation
costs of your LLC:

- **File online:** Most states allow online filing,
  which can be cheaper than paper processing.
- **Act as your own registered agent:** If you have
  a reliable business address and are comfortable
  receiving legal documents, you can save money
  by acting as your own registered agent.
- **Shop around for registered agent services:**
  Compare prices and features before choosing a
  service.

By understanding these costs and employing these
cost–saving strategies, you can keep the formation
process of your LLC affordable.

*In the next sub-chapter,   we'll explore the age-old
question: should you tackle the formation process yourself or seek professional help? We'll weigh the pros and
cons of each approach to help you make the most cost-
effective decision for your LLC.*

C. DIY vs. Professional Help Weighing the Options (Cost vs Expertise)

Now that you're familiar with the costs associated with forming an LLC, it's time to decide whether to tackle the process yourself or enlist the help of a professional. Both options have merits and drawbacks, and the most cost-effective choice depends on your specific circumstances.

The Do-It-Yourself (DIY) Approach:

Going the DIY route can be a significant cost-saver. There are numerous online resources and formation services that offer step-by-step guidance for filing the necessary paperwork.

Benefits of DIY:

- **Cost-effective:** This is undoubtedly the most budget-friendly option. You'll only pay for the filing fees and any optional services you choose (like registered agent services).
- **Sense of accomplishment:** Completing the formation process yourself can be a rewarding experience, fostering a sense of ownership and control over your business.

Drawbacks of DIY:

- **Risk of errors:** Navigating legal and tax regulations can be complex. Mistakes during filing can lead to delays or even rejection of your LLC formation.

- **Time commitment:** Researching and completing the formation process can be time-consuming, especially if you're unfamiliar with business legalities.

Seeking Professional Help:

Hiring a lawyer or business formation service can provide valuable peace of mind and ensure everything is done correctly.

Benefits of Professional Help:

- **Expertise:** Professionals can guide you through the intricacies of LLC formation, ensuring all legal requirements are met.
- **Time-saving:** They can handle the paperwork and filings, freeing you to focus on other aspects of launching your business.
- **Potential for long-term guidance:** Many professionals offer ongoing legal and tax advice, which can be invaluable as your business grows.

Drawbacks of Professional Help:

- **Cost:** Hiring a lawyer or service can add a significant expense to the formation process. Fees can vary depending on the complexity of your business and the experience of the professional.

Choosing the Right Option for You:

If you're comfortable with navigating legal documents and have a limited budget, the DIY approach might be a good fit. However, if you're unsure about the process, value your time, or have a complex business structure, then seeking professional help could be a wise investment.

Here are some additional factors to consider when making your decision:

- **The complexity of your business:** If your business has multiple members, complex ownership structures, or operates in a highly regulated industry, professional help might be advisable.
- **Your comfort level with legal matters:** If legal jargon makes your head spin, then consulting a professional can provide much-needed clarity and peace of mind.
- **Your available time:** If you're short on time to devote to research and paperwork, then a professional service can streamline the process.

No matter which path you choose, the next sub-chapter will equip you with valuable resources to navigate the formation process, whether you go DIY or seek

D. Finding Free and Low-Cost Resources (Government Websites, Legal Aid Programs)

Congratulations on taking charge of your LLC formation! Whether you've chosen the DIY route or are considering professional help, having access to free and low-cost resources is crucial for navigating the process efficiently and cost-effectively.   This sub-chapter will equip you with valuable tools to streamline your LLC formation journey.

Government Websites:
   A treasure trove of information awaits you on the websites of your state's Secretary of State and the U.S. Small Business Administration (SBA). Here's what you can expect to find:

   - **Secretary of State Websites:**Most state government websites offer dedicated sections for forming an LLC. These sections typically provide step-by-step instructions, downloadable forms, and fee information.
   - **U.S. Small Business Administration (SBA):** The SBA website offers a wealth of resources for entrepreneurs, including guides on forming and

managing an LLC. They also provide a directory of local Small Business Development Centers (SBDCs) that offer free or low-cost business counseling.

Legal Aid Programs:

Many states offer legal aid programs that can provide free or low-cost assistance with forming an LLC. These programs often cater to low-income entrepreneurs and can be a valuable resource for getting your business off the ground.

Online Resources:

The internet offers a plethora of free and low-cost resources for forming an LLC. Here are a few reputable options to explore:

- **U.S. Legal Services Corporation (LSC):** The LSC website offers a directory of legal aid programs by state, including those specializing in business law.
- **SCORE:** SCORE is a non-profit organization that connects experienced business mentors with aspiring entrepreneurs. SCORE mentors can provide valuable guidance on forming and managing your LLC.
- **Nolo:** Nolo is a legal publisher that offers a variety of resources for forming an LLC, including online articles, downloadable forms, and self-

help books.

Additional Tips:

- **Law libraries:** Many public libraries have law libraries that offer access to legal resources and assistance from librarians who can help you find the information you need.
- **Business incubators and co-working spaces:** These facilities often offer workshops and resources on forming and running a business.

By leveraging these free and low-cost resources, you can gain the knowledge and confidence to navigate the LLC formation process, even on a budget. In the final sub-chapter of Chapter 1, we'll explore the art of the hustle – creative strategies for saving money on LLC formation services and legal fees.

E. The Art of the Hustle—Creative Strategies for Saving Money (Bartering, Online Tools)

So you've embraced the DIY approach to LLC formation and you're ready to tackle the process like a resourceful entrepreneur. This sub-chapter will equip you with some creative strategies, or "hustles," to minimize costs and maximize your budget during formation.

Barter Your Skills:

Do you possess valuable skills that others might need? Consider bartering your expertise for services related to LLC formation. For instance, if you're a graphic designer, you could offer to create a logo for a lawyer in exchange for a consultation on LLC legalities.

Look for Student Discounts:

Some legal and business service providers offer discounts to students. If you're currently enrolled in a relevant program, like business or paralegal studies, inquire about student discounts for LLC formation services.

Utilize Online Tools and Templates:

Several online legal document creation platforms offer free or low-cost templates for LLC formation documents, such as Articles of Organization and Operating Agreements. While these templates can be a valuable starting point, remember they may not be customized for your specific needs. It's always wise to consult with a legal professional to ensure everything is in order.

Become a Weekend Warrior:

Many online resources and formation services offer free trials or introductory periods. Take advantage of these by dedicating focused weekends to researching the process and completing paperwork during these trial periods.

Network with Other Entrepreneurs:

Connect with other entrepreneurs in your community. They may have valuable insights and recommendations for cost-effective LLC formation services or resources they've discovered.

Embrace the Power of Negotiation:

Don't be afraid to negotiate fees with potential registered agent services or other business formation service providers. Explain your budget and see if they're willing to offer a discount or create a customized package that fits your needs.

Remember, the key to effective hustling is resourcefulness and creativity. By thinking outside the box and leveraging these strategies, you can significantly reduce the costs associated with forming your LLC.

Congratulations! You've completed Chapter 1: Building Your Foundation on a Budget.   In the next chapter, we'll

2

Keeping Your Business Lean and Mean

A. Location (Home Office vs Coworking Spaces vs. Traditional Office)

In Chapter 1, we focused on building a rock-solid foundation for your LLC on a budget.   Now, let's shift gears and explore strategies for keeping your business "lean and mean" throughout its lifecycle. This chapter will equip you with essential tools to minimize overhead costs and maximize efficiency, ensuring your startup thrives without breaking the bank.

   Our first order of business? Finding the perfect home for your business operations - your workspace. The right workspace can significantly impact your budget, productivity, and overall business culture.

This sub-chapter will   delve into the three main options for housing your LLC:

- **The Home Office:**

The home office is a classic choice for budget-conscious startups.   It offers the ultimate in flexibility and convenience, allowing you to work from the comfort of your own home.

  - **Pros:**
  - **Cost-effective:** You eliminate the overhead costs associated with traditional office space, such as rent, utilities, and janitorial services.
  - **Flexible work schedule:** Working from home allows you to create a work schedule that suits your needs and lifestyle.
  - **Minimal commute:** Say goodbye to traffic jams and long commutes!
  - **Cons:**
  - **Work-life balance challenges:** Blending your personal and professional lives can be tricky.
  - **Potential distractions:** Household chores, family members, and pets can disrupt your workday.
  - **Limited professional image:** A home office might not project the professional image you desire, especially if you meet clients in person.
  - **Coworking Spaces:**

Coworking spaces offer a shared work environment with other startups and entrepreneurs. This option provides a more professional setting than a home office while remaining cost-effective.

- **Pros:**
- **Affordable:** Coworking spaces offer flexible leasing options, allowing you to pay for the space you need.
- **Networking opportunities:** Coworking spaces foster a collaborative environment, allowing you to connect with other professionals.
- **Amenities:** Many coworking spaces offer amenities like Wi-Fi, printing services, and conference rooms.
- **Cons:**
- **Lack of privacy:** Coworking spaces can be noisy and distracting, making it difficult to concentrate on focused work.
- **Limited control over environment:** You may not have the same level of control over the temperature, lighting, or décor as you would in a traditional office.
- **Potential commitment:** Some coworking spaces require monthly memberships, which can be a financial consideration.
- **Traditional Office Space:**

The traditional office offers a dedicated space for your business, fostering a professional image and allowing for greater control over your work environment.

- **Pros:**
- **Professional image:** A traditional office space projects a professional image to clients and potential investors.
- **Increased productivity:** A dedicated workspace can minimize distractions and enhance focus.
- **Customization:** You can design and customize your office space to meet your specific needs.
- **Cons:**
- **Most expensive option:** Traditional office space comes with the highest overhead costs, including rent, utilities, and maintenance.
- **Less flexibility:** Leases for traditional   office space typically lock you into a long-term commitment.
- **Scalability challenges:** Growing or shrinking your office space can be a complex and costly process.

Choosing the Right Workspace for Your LLC:
The ideal workspace for your LLC depends on several factors, including your budget, business size, and the nature of your work. Consider the pros and

cons of each option carefully to make an informed decision that balances affordability with your needs for professionalism and productivity.

In the next sub-chapter, we'll delve into the exciting world of technology on a budget.   We'll explore free and open-source software solutions and cloud-based tools that can help you streamline your operations and keep costs under control.

B. Technology on a Budget (Free and Open-Source Software, Cloud-Based Solutions)

In today's digital age, technology is essential for any business operation. However, equipping your startup with the latest software and hardware can quickly become a budget buster. This sub-chapter will equip you with savvy strategies for leveraging free and open-source software (FOSS) and cloud-based solutions to keep your tech stack lean and your budget happy.

The Power of Free and Open-Source Software (FOSS):

The world of FOSS offers a treasure trove of power-ful and versatile software applications that are com-pletely free to use and modify. These applications can rival their paid counterparts in functionality and features. Here are some popular FOSS options to consider for your LLC:

- **Operating System:** Instead of shelling out for a commercial operating system, consider Linux distributions like Ubuntu or Mint.   They offer a stable and secure platform for running your business applications.
- **Office Suite:** Ditch expensive office software suites! LibreOffice provides a robust suite of applications for word processing, spreadsheets, presentations, and more.
- **Project Management:** Keep your projects on track with free project management tools like Trello or Asana.
- **Graphic Design:** For basic graphic design needs, explore free options like GIMP, a feature-rich image manipulation program.

The Advantages of FOSS:

- **Cost-effective:** There's no upfront cost or licensing fees associated with FOSS.
- **Customization:** Many FOSS applications offer open-source code, allowing you to tailor them to your specific needs.
- **Security:** With a large community of developers actively contributing, FOSS applications often

benefit from strong security features.

Exploring Cloud-Based Solutions:

Cloud-based solutions offer a cost-effective alternative to traditional software installations.   These solutions store your data and applications on remote servers, accessible from any device with an internet connection. Here are some benefits of cloud-based solutions:

- **Scalability:** Easily scale your storage and applications up or down as your business grows.
- **Accessibility:** Access your data and applications from anywhere, anytime.
- **Reduced IT Costs:** Eliminate the need for expensive hardware and software licenses.

Popular Cloud-Based Solutions for Startups:

- **Email and Collaboration:** Free or low-cost email and collaboration tools like Gmail and Google Drive offer a robust platform for communication and file sharing.
- **Customer Relationship Management (CRM):** Free CRM solutions like Zoho CRM or HubSpot Free allow you to manage customer interactions and relationships.
- **Accounting:** Cloud-based accounting software

like Wave or Zoho Books simplifies bookkeeping
and financial management.

Making the Most of Technology on a Budget:

- **Research and compare:** Take advantage of free
  trials and demos before committing to any software or cloud-based solution.
- **Start simple:** Don't overwhelm yourself with too
  many tools. Begin with a few essential applications and add more as your business grows.
- **Embrace free resources:** There's a wealth of free
  online tutorials and guides available to help you
  learn how to use FOSS and cloud-based solutions
  effectively.

*By leveraging these strategies, you can equip your LLC
with the technological tools it needs to thrive, all while
staying within your budget.   In the next sub-chapter,
we'll   explore the exciting world of   marketing on a
shoestring – exploring free and low-cost strategies to
get your brand noticed without breaking the bank.*

C. Marketing Without Breaking the Bank (Social Media, Content Marketing)

Marketing is essential for any business, but for budget-conscious startups, traditional advertising can seem out of reach. Fear not! The digital age offers a wealth of free and low-cost marketing tools and strategies to get your brand noticed and attract customers. This sub-chapter will explore some of the most effective tactics:

The Power of Social Media:
  Social media platforms like Facebook, Twitter, and Instagram are powerful tools for connecting with your target audience and building brand awareness. Here's how you can leverage them effectively:

- **Create engaging content:** Share valuable and informative content that resonates with your ideal customers. This could include blog posts, infographics, videos, or behind-the-scenes glimpses into your business.
- **Run targeted social media ads:** Many social media platforms offer affordable advertising options that allow you to target your ideal customer demographic.
- **Interact with your audience:** Respond to comments and messages promptly, fostering a sense

of community around your brand.

Content Marketing: Building Brand Authority
Content marketing involves creating and sharing valuable content that attracts and engages your target audience. This establishes your brand as an authority in your industry and positions you as a trusted resource for potential customers. Here are some content marketing tactics to consider:

- **Start a blog:** Share insightful and informative blog posts related to your industry. This establishes you as a thought leader and drives organic traffic to your website.
- **Guest blogging:** Contribute guest posts to relevant blogs in your industry. This expands your reach and introduces you to a new audience.
- **Create engaging videos:** Videos are a powerful way to capture attention and convey information. Share informative or entertaining videos on social media or your website.

Maximizing the Impact of Your Marketing Efforts:

- **Track your results:** Use analytics tools to track the performance of your marketing campaigns. This allows you to identify what's working and adjust your strategy accordingly.

- **Focus on essential needs:** By saying "no" to unnecessary expenses, you can allocate resources towards critical investments for your business.
- **Informed decision-making:** Developing a prioritization framework helps you make wise financial choices for your LLC.

Developing a Prioritization Framework:

1. **Identify your goals:** Clearly define your short-term and long-term goals for your LLC. This helps you understand what resources you need to achieve them.
2. **Categorize your expenses:** Classify your business expenses into essential (rent, utilities, payroll), important but flexible (marketing costs, travel), and non-essential (subscriptions you rarely use, expensive office supplies).
3. **Evaluate each expense:** Critically evaluate each expense based on its contribution to your business goals. Can the expense be reduced, eliminated, or replaced with a more cost-effective alternative?
4. **Learn to say "no":** Don't be afraid to decline unnecessary purchases or subscriptions. Explain your decision politely and focus on prioritizing essential expenses for your LLC's growth.

Benefits of Saying "No":

- **Reduced financial burden:** By eliminating unnecessary expenses, you free up resources for more critical investments.
- **Increased efficiency:** Focusing on essential spending encourages resourceful and cost-effective solutions for your business needs.
- **Empowers informed decision-making:** Saying "no" fosters a mindset of financial responsibility, leading to more informed decisions about resource allocation.

The Power of Resourcefulness:

There are countless ways to be resourceful when running a lean startup. Here are some ideas:

- **Barter your services:** Offer your skills or expertise in exchange for services your LLC needs.
- **Negotiate with vendors:** Don't be afraid to negotiate for better pricing on services and supplies.
- **Utilize free resources:** Take advantage of the wealth of free online tools and resources available to entrepreneurs.

Saying "no" isn't about shutting down opportunities; it's about making informed choices that propel your LLC towards sustainable growth. By prioritizing spending, developing a clear framework for financial decisions, and embracing resourcefulness, you can empower your business to thrive without unnecessary financial burdens.

3

Long-Term Strategies for Financial Success

A. Setting Up Your Business Finances (Bank Accounts, Basic Bookkeeping)

Just like a sturdy building needs a solid foundation, a successful LLC requires a strong financial foundation. This sub-chapter equips you with the essential knowledge to establish a financial system for your business, including setting up dedicated bank accounts and implementing basic bookkeeping practices.

Separate Your Business and Personal Finances:

- **Business Bank Account:** Opening a dedicated business bank account separates your business

income and expenses from your personal finances. This simplifies record-keeping, clarifies
tax filing, and demonstrates professionalism.
- **Benefits of a Business Bank Account:**
- **Clearer Financial Picture:** Tracks your business
income and outgoings distinctly.
- **Simplified Tax Filing:** Separates business transactions for accurate tax reporting.
- **Professional Image:** Projects a professional
image to clients, investors, and creditors.

Choosing the Right Bank Account:

- **Consider your needs:** Research and compare dif-
ferent business bank accounts offered by various
banks. Factors to consider include monthly fees,
minimum balance requirements, transaction
limits, and online banking features.
- **Common Business Bank Account Types:**
- **Business Checking Account:** Ideal for everyday
business transactions like receiving payments
and making bill payments.
- **Business Savings Account:** Earns interest on
your business savings and can be used for building an emergency fund or saving for future investments.

Understanding Basic Bookkeeping Practices:

Bookkeeping is the process of recording your business's financial transactions. While robust accounting software exists,   grasping basic bookkeeping principles empowers you to manage your finances effectively.

- **The Importance of Bookkeeping:**
- **Tracks Financial Performance:** Monitor income, expenses, and profitability to make informed business decisions.
- **Ensures Tax Compliance:** Accurate bookkeeping forms the basis for filing accurate tax returns.
- **Provides Financial Insights:** Financial records reveal trends and patterns, allowing you to identify areas for improvement or cost savings.
- **Basic Bookkeeping Practices:**
- **Track Income and Expenses:** Maintain meticulous records of all your business income (sales, service fees) and expenses (rent, supplies, payroll).
- **Categorize Transactions:** Classify your income and expenses into relevant categories for easy analysis.
- **Reconcile Your Accounts Regularly:** Regularly compare your bank account statements with your bookkeeping records to ensure accuracy.

Moving Forward:

By establishing dedicated business bank accounts and implementing basic bookkeeping practices, you've laid the groundwork for strong financial management. In the next sub-chapter, we'll delve into the art of budgeting and cash flow management, crucial tools for navigating the financial landscape of your LLC.

B. Taxes on a Budget (Understanding Your Tax Obligations, Free Tax Filing Resources)

Taxes are a fact of life for every business owner. While they may not be exciting, understanding your tax obligations and incorporating them into your budget is crucial for financial stability and avoiding surprises come tax season. This sub-chapter equips you with the knowledge to navigate the world of LLC taxes and budget for them effectively.

Understanding Your Tax Obligations:

The type of taxes your LLC is liable for depends on its business structure and how you choose to be taxed. Here's a general overview:

- **Federal Income Tax:** Most LLCs are considered "pass-through entities." This means the business itself doesn't pay income tax. Instead, the profits or losses of the LLC "pass through" to the owner(s) and are reported on their personal income tax returns.

- **Self-Employment Tax:** In addition to federal income tax, LLC owners must pay self-employment tax. This covers Social Security and Medicare contributions.
- **State and Local Taxes:**Your LLC may also be subject to state and local taxes, which vary depending on your location. These may include sales tax, unemployment tax, or franchise taxes.

It's important to consult with a tax professional to determine the specific tax obligations of your LLC. They can guide you based on your business structure, location, and income.

Budgeting for Taxes:

Taxes are a significant expense, so it's crucial to factor them into your LLC's budget. Here's how to approach budgeting for taxes:

- **Estimate your annual tax liability:** Work with your tax professional to estimate your federal income tax, self-employment tax, and any applicable state or local taxes.
- **Set aside funds throughout the year:** Don't wait until tax season to scramble for funds. Regularly allocate a portion of your income into a separate savings account earmarked for taxes.

- **Consider quarterly tax payments:**For some LLCs, especially those with significant income, quarterly estimated tax payments may be required. Consult your tax professional to determine if this applies to your business.

Free Tax Filing Resources:
The IRS and many states offer free tax filing resources for small businesses and individuals with modest incomes. Here are some resources to explore:

- **IRS Free File:**The IRS Free File program connects taxpayers with a variety of free tax filing software options. (https://www.irs.gov/filing/free-file-do-your-federal-taxes-for-free)
- **Volunteer Income Tax Assistance (VITA):** The VITA program offers free tax preparation assistance to low- to moderate-income taxpayers. ([URLVITA free tax help ON IRS (.gov) irs.gov])

By understanding your tax obligations, incorporating them into your budget, and leveraging available resources, you can approach tax season with confidence and ensure your LLC remains financially sound.

C. Building Business Credit (Establishing Relationships with Vendors, Managing Debt Wisely)

As your LLC flourishes,   building strong business credit becomes increasingly important. Good business credit allows you to access financing for future growth, secure favorable payment terms with vendors, and potentially qualify for lower insurance premiums. This sub-chapter equips you with strategies to establish and cultivate business credit while fostering healthy financial habits.

Establishing Relationships with Vendors:
Building relationships with vendors is a cornerstone of establishing business credit. Here's how to make a positive impression:

- **Pay invoices on time:** Demonstrate your credit-worthiness by paying invoices promptly according to the agreed-upon terms.
- **Maintain clear communication:** Proactively communicate any delays or challenges regarding invoice payments.
- **Negotiate favorable terms:** As your business grows and your payment history strengthens, negotiate extended payment terms or discounts with vendors.

Building a Business Credit History:

- **Obtain a business tax ID:** A business tax ID, also known as an Employer Identification Number (EIN), is essential for establishing business credit. It differentiates your business from your personal finances.
- **Open a business credit card:** Utilize a business credit card responsibly and pay your balances in full each month to build a positive credit history.
- **Apply for a business loan:** Consider applying for a small business loan and repaying it diligently. This demonstrates your ability to manage debt responsibly.

Managing Debt Wisely:

Debt can be a powerful tool for growth, but it needs to be managed wisely. Here are some principles to consider:

- **Borrow only what you can afford to repay:** Carefully assess your financial situation before taking on debt. Ensure you have a plan for repayment that aligns with your business income.
- **Explore alternative financing options:** Consider alternative financing options like business grants, crowdfunding, or angel investors before resorting to high-interest loans.

- **Monitor your credit reports regularly:** Regularly monitor your business credit reports to ensure accuracy and identify any potential issues that might need to be addressed.

Building business credit is a gradual process, but by establishing positive relationships with vendors, managing debt responsibly, and utilizing available credit-building tools, you can empower your LLC to access financing opportunities that fuel future growth.

D. Rainy Day Funds and Growth Strategies (Saving for Unexpected Expenses, Reinvesting Profits)

Every business owner faces unforeseen challenges. Building a financial safety net and having a plan for reinvesting profits are essential for ensuring your LLC's long-term stability and growth. This sub-chapter equips you with strategies for navigating financial fluctuations and fostering sustainable business expansion.

Building a Safety Net (Rainy Day Fund):

Unexpected expenses are a reality for every business. A rainy day fund, also known as an emergency fund, serves as a financial buffer to weather unexpected challenges.

- **Importance of a Rainy Day Fund:**
- **Covers unexpected expenses:** Prepares you for emergencies like equipment failure, sudden repairs, or economic downturns.
- **Reduces financial stress:** Provides peace of mind knowing you have resources to address unforeseen circumstances.
- **Maintains business continuity:** Ensures your business operations can continue even during challenging times.
- **How Much to Save:** There's no one-size-fits-all answer. Ideally, aim to save 3-6 months of your operating expenses to cover potential shortfalls.

Strategies for Building Your Rainy Day Fund:

- **Allocate a portion of your profits:** Set aside a specific percentage of your income regularly towards your rainy day fund.
- **Identify cost-saving opportunities:** Continuously evaluate your spending and implement cost-saving measures to free up additional resources for your emergency fund.
- **Consider separate accounts:** Open a high-yield savings account specifically for your rainy day fund to avoid the temptation of dipping into

these critical reserves.

Reinvesting Profits for Growth:

While saving for a rainy day is crucial, reinvesting a portion of your profits back into your LLC fuels sustainable growth. Here are some strategic ways to reinvest your profits:

- **Invest in marketing and advertising:** Attract new customers and expand your reach through targeted marketing campaigns.
- **Upgrade equipment and technology:** Invest in modern equipment and technology to improve efficiency and productivity.
- **Invest in your employees:** Provide training and development opportunities to empower your team and enhance their skillsets.
- **Expand your product or service offerings:** Consider introducing new products or services that cater to a wider audience or address evolving customer needs.

The Art of Balancing Savings and Growth:

Finding the right balance between saving for unforeseen circumstances and reinvesting in growth is key. Regularly evaluate your financial situation and adjust your strategy as needed.

Remember, a well-funded LLC is a resilient LLC.

By establishing a safety net through a rainy day fund and implementing strategic reinvestment plans, you can navigate challenges with confidence and propel your business towards a prosperous future.

E. The Bootstrapper's Mindset (Embracing Resourcefulness, Celebrating Small Wins)

The path to entrepreneurial success isn't always filled with venture capital funding and million-dollar budgets. Many LLCs flourish by embracing a bootstrapper's mindset – resourcefulness, creativity, and perseverance in the face of limited resources. This sub-chapter equips you with the tools and strategies to thrive as a bootstrapping entrepreneur, celebrating every milestone along the way.

The Essence of the Bootstrapper's Mindset:

- **Resourcefulness:** Bootstrappers make the most of what they have. They find creative solutions to challenges and leverage free or low-cost tools and resources whenever possible.
- **Focus on Organic Growth:** Bootstrapping businesses prioritize organic growth strategies like building a loyal customer base and reinvesting profits back into the business.
- **Resilience:** The entrepreneurial journey is rarely

smooth sailing. Bootstrappers embrace challenges, learn from setbacks, and persist in the face of adversity.

Benefits of Bootstrapping:

- **Maintains Ownership Control:** Bootstrapping allows you to maintain greater control over your business decisions and overall direction.
- **Financial Discipline:** The need to be resourceful fosters a culture of financial responsibility and cost-effectiveness within your LLC.
- **Increased Value:** Bootstrapped businesses that achieve success are often seen as more valuable by potential investors due to their profitability and proven ability to operate lean.

Strategies for the Bootstrapping Entrepreneur:

- **Embrace Free Resources:** There's a wealth of free online tools and resources available for entrepreneurs, from website building platforms to marketing templates.
- **Barter Your Skills and Services:** Offer your expertise or services in exchange for something your LLC needs, like marketing or legal consultations.
- **Build Relationships and Collaborate:** Network

with other entrepreneurs and explore collaboration opportunities to leverage each other's strengths and resources.

Celebrating Milestones (The Power of Recognition):

The journey of a bootstrapping entrepreneur is paved with small wins. Taking the time to celebrate these milestones keeps you motivated and fosters a sense of accomplishment.

- **Acknowledge Your Achievements:** Recognize and celebrate even the seemingly small wins, like securing your first customer or achieving a sales target.
- **Reward Yourself:** Set milestones and reward yourself for achieving them. This reinforces positive behaviors and keeps you motivated along the way.
- **Share Your Successes:** Share your accomplishments with your team, loved ones, or fellow entrepreneurs. This can boost morale and generate positive momentum.

The bootstrapper's mindset is a powerful asset for any entrepreneur. By embracing resourcefulness, perseverance, and celebrating your wins, you can establish a thriving LLC and pave the way for long-term success.

Congratulations!   You've completed Chapter 3. We've covered a vast array of strategies to ensure your LLC is resilient, adaptable, and well-positioned for long-term success.

4

Conclusion

Congratulations! You've reached the culmination of this guide, equipping yourself with the knowledge and tools to navigate the exciting world of LLC formation and operation. Throughout this book, we've emphasized strategies to empower you, the entrepreneur, to build a resilient, adaptable, and cost-effective business.

We began by demystifying the LLC structure, guiding you through the formation process and highlighting its advantages for aspiring business owners. Chapter 2 focused on establishing a strong financial foundation, emphasizing cost-saving tactics and best practices for managing your LLC's finances. Chapter 3 delved into strategies for building a future-proof business, from prioritizing financial stability and fostering a strong team culture to leveraging technology for growth.

This book consistently emphasized the importance of a cost-conscious approach. We explored strategies for finding free or low-cost resources for legal and tax advice, implementing financial management practices to minimize overhead, and utilizing readily available technology to streamline operations.

As you embark on your entrepreneurial journey, remember these key takeaways:

- **Financial Responsibility is Paramount:** Developing a budget, managing cash flow effectively, and understanding your tax obligations are crucial for long-term financial health.
- **Embrace Resourcefulness:** There's a wealth of free and affordable tools and information at your disposal. Leverage these resources to navigate legal and financial aspects of running your LLC.
- **Invest in Your Team:** A skilled, motivated, and engaged team is the backbone of any successful business.
- **Celebrate Your Wins:** Acknowledge your achievements, big and small, to stay motivated and celebrate your progress on the path to success.

Remember, the road to entrepreneurial success is paved with learning and adaptation. This book has equipped you with a strong foundation, but the journey continues. Embrace challenges as opportunities for growth, stay curious, and continuously seek knowledge to refine your strategies. With dedication, perseverance, and the tools outlined within these pages, you can turn your LLC dream into a thriving reality.

We wish you the very best on your entrepreneurial journey!

www.ingramcontent.com/pod-product-compliance
Lightning Source LLC
Chambersburg PA
CBHW072328270726

48658CB00016B/2056